W9-BUS-682

SATURN

by L. L. Owens

Central Islip Public Library

3 1800 00279 8441

Published by The Child's World®
1980 Lookout Drive • Mankato, MN 56003-1705
800-599-READ • www.childsworld.com

ACKNOWLEDGMENTS
The Child's World®: Mary Berendes, Publishing Director
The Design Lab: Design and production
Red Line Editorial: Editorial direction

PHOTO CREDITS
NASA and E. Karkoschka (University of Arizona)/courtesy of nasaimages.org, cover, 1, 32; NASA/courtesy of nasaimages.org, cover, 1, 3, 6, 11, 12, 16, 28, 29, 31; Francisco Kjolseth/AP Images, 5; NASA/courtesy of nasaimages.org/The Design Lab, 6, 7; NASA and E. Karkoschka (University of Arizona)/courtesy of nasaimages.org/The Design Lab, 9; The Print Collector/Photolibrary, 13; NASA/NSSDC/Catalog of Spaceborne Imaging, 15, 17; AP Images, 19, 25; NASA Jet Propulsion Lab/AP Images, 21; NASA/JPL/Space Science Institute/courtesy of nasaimages.org, 23; NASA/AP Images, 27

Copyright © 2011 by The Child's World®
All rights reserved. No part of this book may be reproduced or utilized in any form or by any means without written permission from the publisher.

LIBRARY OF CONGRESS CATALOGING-IN-PUBLICATION DATA
Owens, L. L.
Saturn / by L. L. Owens.
p. cm.
Includes bibliographical references and index.
ISBN 978-1-60954-387-7 (library bound : alk. paper)
1. Saturn (Planet)—Juvenile literature. I. Title.
QB671.O94 2011
523.46–dc22
2010039964

Printed in the United States of America
Mankato, MN
December, 2010
PA02072

ON THE COVER
Saturn's colorful rings are shown in this image.

Table of Contents

Saturn and the Solar System

Look up at the sky on a clear, starry night. Can you pick out a few of the brightest objects? One of those is Saturn!

Saturn is one of our space neighbors in the **solar system**. At the center of our solar system is the sun. Planets go around, or **orbit**, the sun.

Saturn is seen from
Utah in 2004.

SUN

Mercury
Venus
Earth
Mars
Ceres
Jupiter

Fun Facts

PLANET NUMBER: Saturn is the sixth planet from the sun.

DISTANCE FROM SUN: 886 million miles (1.4 billion km)

SIZE: Saturn is about 235,300 miles (378,700 km) around its middle. That's more than nine times bigger than Earth's middle.

OUR SOLAR SYSTEM: Our solar system has eight planets and five **dwarf planets**. Pluto used to be called a planet. But in 2006, scientists decided to call it a dwarf planet instead. Scientists hope to discover even more dwarf planets in our solar system!

Our Solar System
Saturn
Uranus
Neptune
Pluto
Haumea
Makemake
Eris
Planet
Dwarf Planet

While orbiting the sun, a planet spins like a top. Each planet spins, or rotates, on its **axis**. An axis is an imaginary line that runs through the planet from top to bottom. One full spin on the axis equals one day. Think of one day on a planet as the time from one sunrise to the next sunrise.

A day on Earth is 24 hours. A day on Saturn is only 11 hours! In our solar system, only Jupiter has a shorter day.

An axis runs through the center of a planet. The planet spins on the axis.

One year is the time it takes for a planet to travel once around the sun. A year on Earth is about 365 days. But Saturn travels much more slowly. It takes Saturn about 10,759 days to go around the sun. That's almost 30 Earth years!

Saturn travels slowly around the sun, a ball of glowing **gas** at the center of our solar system.

Viewing Saturn

More than 2,000 years ago, Romans studied the sky. They **observed** the sun, the moon, and the brightest planets. Saturn is the second-biggest planet after Jupiter. Romans named it after their god of farmers—Saturn.

Fun Fact

Uranus (YOOR-uh-nuss) is the seventh planet from the sun. It was discovered in 1781. Until then, people thought Saturn was the last planet in our solar system.

In the 1740s, **astronomers** in Paris used **telescopes** to study Saturn and other objects in the night sky.

Saturn's Moons

As Saturn orbits the sun, moons orbit Saturn. Scientists have counted at least 60 moons around the planet. The largest one is Titan. It is half the size of Earth and bigger than the planet Mercury! Titan has a rocky surface with volcanoes, sand dunes, and lakes of liquid gas.

Scientists think Titan shares many features with Earth.

Layers of Gas

Saturn is a gas giant. Other planets have hard, rocky surfaces. But Saturn has no hard surface. It is made of layers of gas and liquid.

Fun Fact

There are two types of planets.

TERRESTRIAL PLANETS (mostly rock) are close to the sun. They are: Mercury, Venus, Earth, and Mars.

GAS GIANTS (mostly gas and liquid) are farther from the sun. They are: Jupiter, Saturn, Uranus, and Neptune.

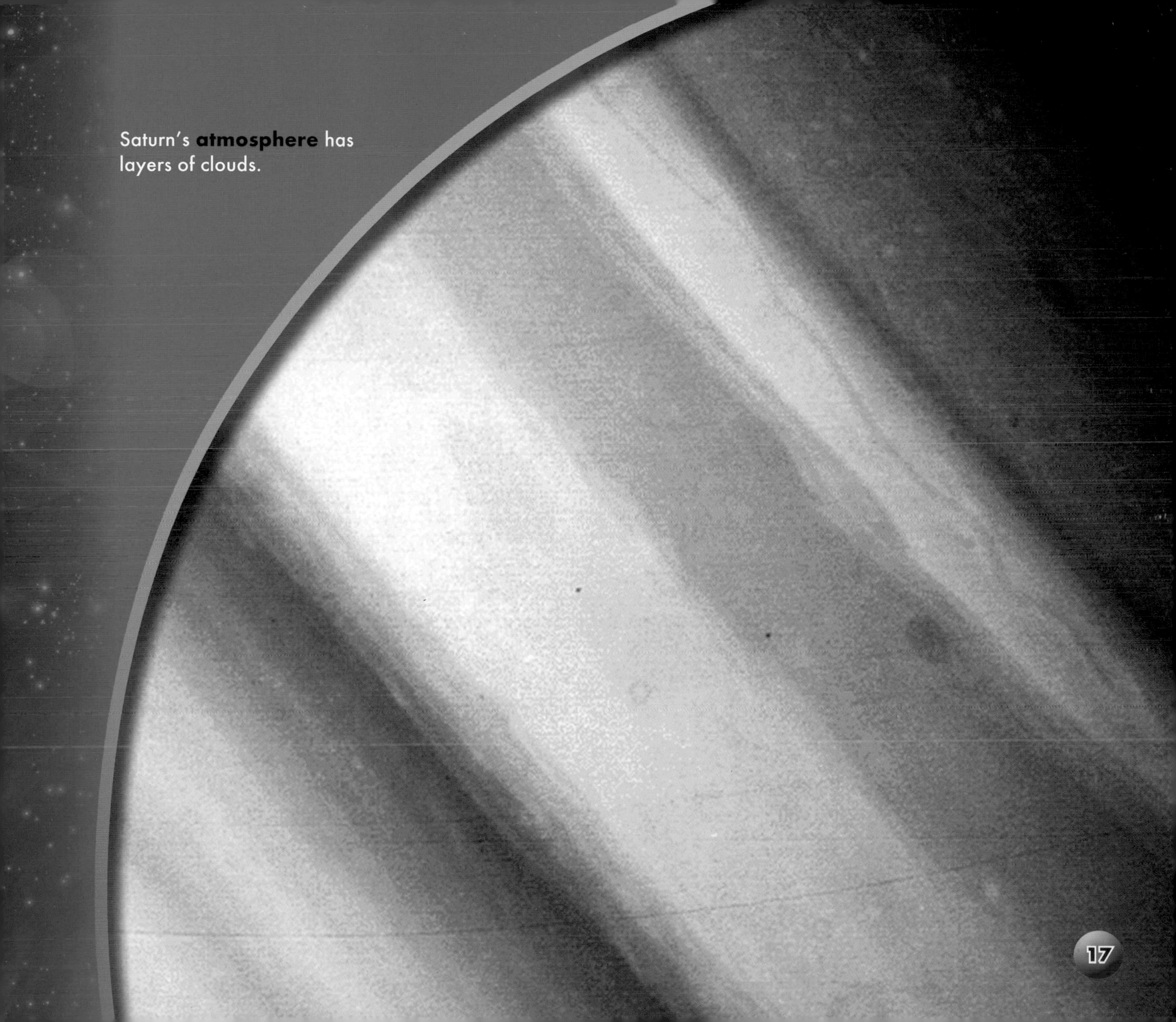

Saturn's **atmosphere** has
layers of clouds.

Beautiful Rings

Saturn is known for its colorful rings. There are too many to count! You need a telescope to see the rings from Earth.

Italian astronomer Galileo Galilei discovered Saturn's rings in 1610. He viewed them with an early telescope, but he didn't know what they were. Scientists now know that Saturn's rings are made of ice. They never touch the planet.

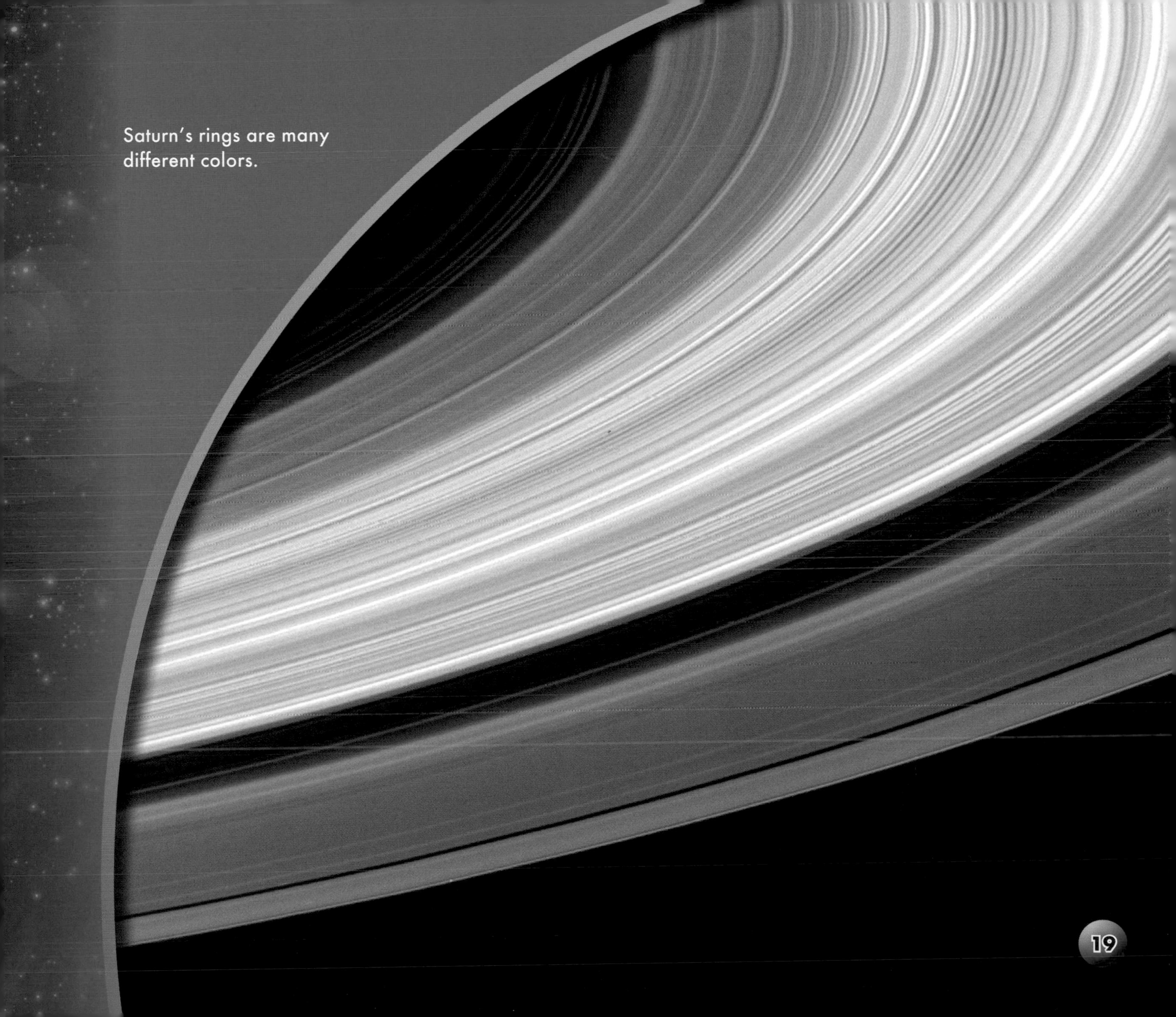

Saturn's rings are many different colors.

Yellow Planet

In space, Saturn looks like a pale yellow ball. The color comes from the planet's atmosphere. An atmosphere is the layer of gas around a planet. Earth's atmosphere is the air we breathe.

Even though Saturn is a gas giant, scientists wonder if there are solids at its center. Saturn is so far from Earth that it is difficult to study.

This image of Saturn was taken by the *Voyager* 2 spacecraft in 1981.

Water and Weather

All life as we know it needs water. Only tiny amounts of water have been found in Saturn's atmosphere. Scientists believe conditions on the planet are too harsh for life to exist.

But one of Saturn's moons, Enceladus (en-SELL-ah-dus), has an icy surface. Scientists believe an ocean is underneath that icy crust. This would make Enceladus one of the few places in our solar system with liquid water!

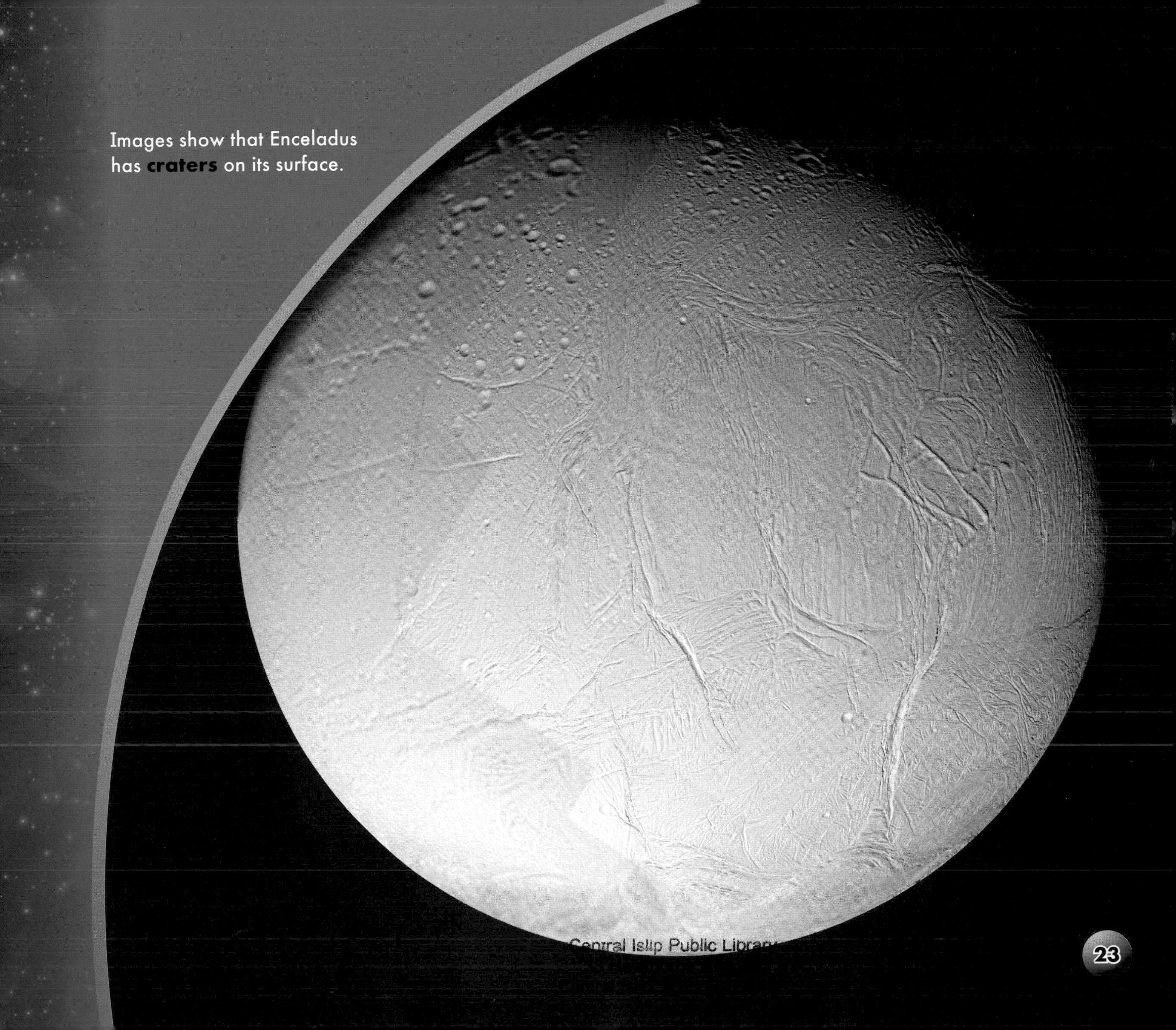

Images show that Enceladus has **craters** on its surface.

Central Islip Public Library

Saturn's distance from the sun makes it a cold planet. Temperatures can dip to –357°F (–216°C). You would freeze solid at that temperature, just like an ice cube!

Saturn's axis is tilted, like Earth's. When one part of the planet is tilted toward the sun, the other part is tilted away.

Saturn's tilt gives the planet its seasons.

Saturn is very stormy. In 2010, a huge storm raged. It was so large, people could see the storm from Earth.

Winds under Saturn's thick, foggy atmosphere can reach 1,000 miles per hour (1,600 km/h). That's three times the speed of Earth's most dangerous tornadoes. And Saturn's lightning can be 10,000 times stronger than lightning on our planet.

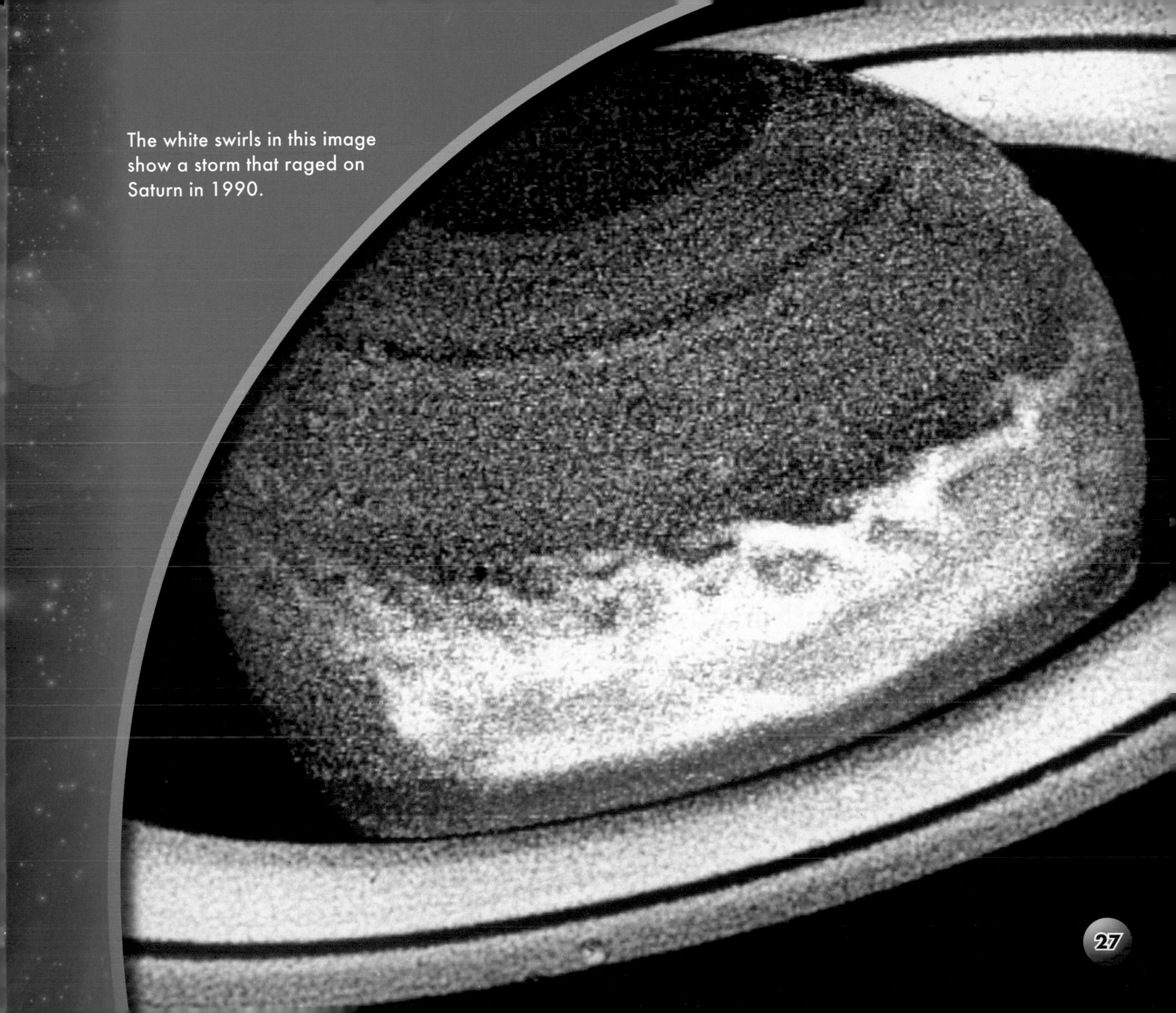

The white swirls in this image show a storm that raged on Saturn in 1990.

Exploring the Planet

NASA's *Cassini* spacecraft studies Saturn. It launched in 1997 and began circling Saturn in 2004. In early 2010, it had already taken 210,000 pictures!

Cassini and other spacecraft will also study some of Saturn's moons. Scientists hope to find liquid water on Enceladus and Titan.

Fun Fact

NASA stands for the National Aeronautics and Space Administration. It is a US agency that studies space and the planets.

Scientists work on the *Cassini* spacecraft in 1997.

GLOSSARY

astronomers (uh-STRON-uh-merz): Astronomers are people who study planets, stars, or moons. Astronomers have studied Saturn for hundreds of years.

atmosphere (AT-muhss-fihr): An atmosphere is the mixture of gases around a planet or a star. Saturn's atmosphere has thick clouds.

axis (AK-siss): An axis is an imaginary line that runs through the center of a planet or a moon. Saturn rotates on its axis.

craters (KRAY-turz): Craters are large areas on the surface of a moon or a planet that dip down, like bowls. Enceladus, one of Saturn's moons, has craters on its surface.

dwarf planets (DWORF PLAN-itz): Dwarf planets are round bodies in space that orbit the sun, are not moons, and are not large enough to clear away their paths around the sun. Dwarf planets often have similar objects that orbit near them.

gas (GASS): A gas is a substance that moves around freely and can spread out. Saturn is made of layers of gas and liquid.

observed (uhb-ZURVD): If something is observed, it is watched and studied closely. People who lived thousands of years ago observed the skies and saw Saturn.

orbit (OR-bit): To orbit is to travel around another body in space, often in an oval path. Planets orbit the sun.

solar system (SOH-lur SISS-tum): Our solar system is made up of the sun, eight planets and their moons, and smaller bodies that orbit the sun. Saturn is the sixth planet from the sun in our solar system.

telescopes (TEL-uh-skohps): Telescopes are tools for making faraway objects appear closer. Scientists use telescopes to see Saturn's rings.

FURTHER INFORMATION

BOOKS

Jefferis, David. *Mighty Megaplanets: Jupiter and Saturn*. New York: Crabtree Publishing, 2009.

Landau, Elaine. *Saturn*. New York: Children's Press, 2008.

Trammel, Howard K. *The Solar System*. New York: Children's Press, 2010.

WEB SITES

Visit our Web site for links about Saturn: **childsworld.com/links**

Note to Parents, Teachers, and Librarians: We routinely verify our Web links to make sure they are safe and active sites. So encourage your readers to check them out!

INDEX

ABOUT THE AUTHOR

L. L. Owens has been writing books for children since 1998. She writes both fiction and nonfiction and especially loves helping kids explore the world around them.

HM AUG 09 2011 ✓

279 8441

J523. Owens, L.L.
46 Saturn
OWE

$28.72

Central Islip Public Library
33 Hawthorne Avenue
Central Islip, NY 11722-2498

GAYLORD